ON THE FLESH OF CHRIST

Tertullian

Table of Contents

Table of Contents

Table of Contents

ON THE FLESH OF CHRIST

Tertullian

ON THE FLESH OF CHRIST

SCRIPTURE. THOSE WHO ASSAIL THE TRUE DOCTRINE OF THE ONE LORD JESUS CHRIST, BOTH GOD AND MAN, THUS CONDEMNED.
- CHAP. XXV.—CONCLUSION.THIS TREATISE FORMS A PREFACE TO THE OTHER WORK, "ON "PROVING THE RESURRECTION OF THE FLESH," THE REALITY OF THE FLESH WHICH WAS TRULY BORN, AND DIED, AND ROSE AGAIN.
- ELUCIDATIONS.

V. ON THE FLESH OF CHRIST.(1)

THIS WAS WRITTEN BY OUR AUTHOR IN CONFUTATION OF CERTAIN HERETICS WHO DENIED THE REALITY OF CHRIST'S FLESH, OR AT LEAST ITS IDENTITY WITH HUMAN FLESH—FEARING THAT, IF THEY ADMITTED THE REALITY OF CHRIST'S FLESH, THEY MUST ALSO ADMIT HIS RESURRECTION IN THE FLESH; AND, CONSEQUENTLY, THE RESURRECTION OF THE HUMAN BODY AFTER DEATH.

[TRANSLATED BY DR. HOLMES.]

CHAP. I.—THE GENERAL PURPORT OF THIS WORK. THE HERETICS, MARCION, APELLES, AND VALENTINUS, WISHING TO IMPUGN THE DOCTRINE OF THE RESURRECTION, DEPRIVE CHRIST OF ALL CAPACITY FOR SUCH A CHANGE BY DENYING HIS FLESH.

THEY who are so anxious to shake that belief in the resurrection which was firmly settled' before the appearance of our modern Sadducees,(3) as even to deny that the expectation thereof has any relation whatever to the flesh, have great cause for besetting the flesh of Christ also with doubtful questions, as if it either had no existence at all, or possessed a nature altogether different from human flesh. For they cannot but be apprehensive that, if it be once determined that Christ'(4) flesh was human, a presumption would immediately arise in opposition to them, that that flesh must by all means rise again, which has already risen in Christ. Therefore we shall have to guard our belief in the resurrection 4 from the same armoury, whence they get their weapons of destruction. Let us examine our Lord's bodily substance, for about His spiritual nature all are agreed.(5) It is 'His flesh that is in question. Its verity and quality are the points in dispute. Did it ever exist? whence was it derived? and of what kind was it? If we succeed in demonstrating it, we shall lay down a law for our own resurrection. Marcion, in order that he might deny the flesh of Christ, denied also His nativity, or else he denied His flesh in order that he might deny His nativity; because, of course, he was afraid that His nativity and His flesh bore mutual testimony to each other's reality, since there is no nativity without flesh, and no flesh without nativity. As if indeed, under the prompting of that licence which is ever the same in all heresy, he too might not very well have either denied the nativity, although admitting the flesh,—like Apelles, who was first a disciple of his, and afterwards an apostate,—or, while admitting both the flesh and the nativity, have interpreted them in a different sense, as did Valentinus, who resembled Apelles both in his discipleship and desertion of Martian. At all events, he who represented the flesh of Christ to be imaginary was equally able to pass off His nativity as a phantom; so that the virgin's conception, and pregnancy, and child–bearing, and then the whole course(6) of her infant too, would have to be regarded as putative.(7) These facts pertaining to the nativity of Christ would escape the notice of the same eyes and the same senses as failed to grasp the full idea(8) of His flesh.

CHAP. II.—MARCION, WHO WOULD BLOT OUT THE RECORD OF CHRIST'S NATIVITY, IS REBUKED FOR SO STARTLING A HERESY.

Clearly enough is the nativity announced by Gabriel.(1) But what has he to do with the Creator's angel?(2) The conception in the virgin's womb is also set plainly before us. But what concern has he with the Creator's prophet, Isaiah?(3) He(4) will not brook delay, since sudden/y (without any prophetic announcement) did he bring down Christ from heaven.(5) "Away," says he, "with that eternal plaguey taxing of Caesar, and the scanty inn, and the squalid swaddling–clothes, and the hard stable.(6) We do not care a jot for(7) that multitude of the heavenly host which praised their Lord at night? Let the shepherds take better care of their flock,(9) and let the wise men spare their legs so long a journey;(10) let them keep their gold to themselves." Let Herod, too, mend his manners, so that Jeremy may not glory over him.(12) Spare also the babe from circumcision, that he may escape the pain thereof; nor let him be brought into the temple, lest he burden his parents with the expense of the offering;(13) nor let him be handed to Simeon, lest the old man be saddened at the point of death.(14) Let that old woman also hold her tongue, lest she should bewitch the child."(15) After such a fashion as this, I suppose you have had, O Marcion, the hardihood of blotting out the original records (of the history) of Christ that His flesh may lose the proofs of its reality. But, prithee, on what grounds (do you do this)? Show me your authority. If you are a prophet, foretell us a thing; if you are an apostle, open your message in public; if a follower of apostles,(16) side with apostles in thought; if you are only a (private) Christian, believe what has been handed down to us: if, however, you are nothing of all this, then (as I have the best reason to say) cease to live.(17) For indeed you are already dead, since you are no Christian, because you do not believe that which by being believed makes men Christian,—nay, you are the more dead, the more you are not a Christian; having fallen away, after you had been one, by rejecting(18) what you formerly believed, even as you yourself acknowledge in a certain letter of yours, and as your followers do not deny, whilst our (brethren) can prove it.(19) Rejecting, therefore, what you once` believed, you have completed the act of rejection, by now no longer believing: the fact, however, of your having ceased. to believe has not made your rejection of the faith right and proper; nay, rather,(20) by your act of rejection you prove that what you believed previous to the said act was of a different character.(21) What you believed to be of a different character, had been handed down just as you believed it. Now(20) that which had been handed down was true, inasmuch as it had been transmitted by those whose duty it was to hand it down. Therefore, when rejecting that which had been handed down, you rejected that which was true. You had no authority for what you did. However, we have already in another treatise availed ourselves more fully of these prescriptive rules against all heresies. Our repetition of them hereafter that large (treatise) is superfluous,(23) when we ask the reason why you have formed the opinion that Christ was not born.

CHAP. III.—CHRIST'S NATIVITY BOTH POSSIBLE AND BECOMING. THE HERETICAL OPINION OF CHRIST'S APPARENT FLESH DECEPTIVE AND DISHONOURABLE TO GOD, EVEN ON MARCION'S PRINCIPLES.

Since(24) you think that this lay within the competency of your own arbitrary choice, you must needs have supposed that being born(25) was either impossible for God, or unbecoming to Him. With God, however, nothing is impossible but what He does not will. Let us consider, then, whether He willed to be born (for if He had the will, He also had the power, and was born). I put the argument very briefly. If God had willed not to be born, it matters not why, He would not have presented Himself in the likeness of man. Now who, when he sees a man, would deny that he had been born? What God therefore willed not to be, He would in no wise have willed the seeming to be. When a thing is distasteful, the very notion(26) of it is scouted; because it makes no difference whether a thing exist or do not exist, if, when it does not exist, it is yet assumed to exist. It is of course of the greatest importance that there should be nothing false (or pretended) attributed to that which really does not exist.(1) But, say you, His own consciousness (of the truth of His nature) was enough for Him. If any supposed that He had been born, because they saw Him as a man, that was their concern.(2) Yet with how much more dignity and consistency would He have sustained the human character on the supposition that He was truly born; for if He were not born, He could not have undertaken the said character without injury to that consciousness of His which you on your side attribute to His confidence of being able to sustain, although not born, the character of having been born even against! His own consciousness!(3) Why, I want to know,(4) was it of so much importance, that Christ should, when perfectly aware what He really was, exhibit Himself as being that which He was not? You cannot express any apprehension that,s if He had been born and truly clothed Himself with man's nature, He would have ceased to be God, losing what He was, while becoming what He was not. For God is in no danger of losing His own state and condition. But, say you, I deny that God was truly changed to man in such wise as to be born and endued with a body of flesh, on this ground, that a being who is without end is also of necessity incapable of change. For being changed into something else puts an end to the former state. Change, therefore, is not possible to a Being who cannot come to an end. Without doubt, the nature of things which are subject to change is regulated by this law, that they have no permanence in the state which is undergoing change in them, and that they come to an end from thus wanting permanence, whilst they lose that in the process of change which they previously were. But nothing is equal with God; His nature is different(6) from the condition of all things. If, then, the things which differ from God, and from which God differs, lose what existence they had whilst they are undergoing change, wherein will consist the difference of the Divine Being from all other things except in His possessing the contrary faculty of theirs,—in other words, that God can be changed into all conditions, and yet continue just as He is? On any other supposition, He would be on the, same level with those things which, when changed, lose the existence they had before; whose equal, of course, He is not in any other respect, as He certainly is not in the changeful issues(7) of their nature. You have sometimes read and believed that the Creator's angels have been changed into human form, and have even borne about so veritable a body, that Abraham even washed their feet,(8) and Lot was rescued from the Sodomites by their hands;(9) an angel, moreover, wrestled with a man so strenuously with his body, that the latter desired to be let loose, so tightly was he held.(10) Has it, then, been permitted to angels, which are inferior to God, after they have been changed into human bodily form,(11) nevertheless to remain angels? and will you deprive God, their superior, of this faculty, as if Christ could not continue to be God, after His real assumption of the nature of man? Or else, did those angels appear as phantoms of flesh? You will not, however, have the courage to say this; for if it be so held in your belief, that the Creator's angels are in the same condition as Christ, then Christ will belong to the same God as those angels do, who are like Christ in their condition. If you had not purposely rejected in some instances, and corrupter in others, the Scriptures which are opposed to your opinion, you would have been confuted in this matter by the Gospel of John, when it declares that the Spirit descended in the body(12) of a dove, and sat upon the Lord.(13) When the said Spirit was in this condition, He was as truly a dove as He was also a spirit; nor did He destroy His own proper substance by the assumption of an extraneous substance. But you ask what becomes of the dove's body, after the return of the Spirit back to heaven, and similarly in the case of the angels. Their withdrawal was effected in the same manner as their appearance had been. If you had seen how their production out of nothing had been effected, you would have known also the process of their return to nothing. If the initial step was out of sight, so was also the final one. Still there was solidity in their bodily substance, whatever may have been the force by which the body became visible.What is written cannot but have been.

CHAP. IV.—GOD'S HONOUR IN THE INCARNATION OF HIS SON VINDICATED. MARCION'S DISPARAGEMENT OF HUMAN FLESH INCONSISTENT AS WELL AS IMPIOUS. CHRIST HAS CLEANSED THE FLESH.THE FOOLISHNESS OF GOD IS MOST WISE.

Since, therefore, you do not reject the assumption of a body' as impossible or as hazardous to the character of God, it remains for you to repudiate and censure it as unworthy of Him. Come now, beginning from the nativity itself, declaim(2) against the uncleanness of the generative elements within the womb, the filthy concretion of fluid and blood, of the growth of the flesh for nine: months long out of that very mire. Describe the womb as it enlarges(3) from day to day,heavy, troublesome, restless even in sleep, changeful in its feelings of dislike and desire. Inveigh now likewise against the shame itself of a woman in travail(4) which, however, ought rather to be honoured in consideration of that peril, or to be held sacred(5) in respect of (the mystery of) nature. Of course you are horrified also at the infant, which is shed into life with the embarrassments which accompany it from the womb;(6) you likewise, of course, loathe it even after it is washed, when it is dressed out in its swaddling–clothes, graced with repeated anointing,(7) smiled on with nurse's fawns. This reverend course of nature,(8) you, O Marcion, (are pleased to) spit upon; and yet, in what way were you born? You detest a human being at his birth; then after what fashion do you love anybody? Yourself, of course, you had no love of, when you departed from the Church and the faith of Christ. But never mind? if you are not on good terms with yourself, or even if you were born in a way different from other people.

Christ, at any rate, has loved even that man who was condensed in his mother's womb amidst all its uncleannesses, even that man who was brought into life out of the said womb, even that man who was nursed amidst the nurse's simpers.(10) For his sake He came down (from heaven), for his sake He preached, for his sake "He humbled Himself even unto death—the death of the cross."(11) He loved, of course, the being whom He redeemed at so great a cost. If Christ is the Creator's Son, it was with justice that He loved His own (creature); if He comes from another god, His love was excessive, since He redeemed a being who belonged to another. Well, then, loving man He loved his nativity also, and his flesh as well. Nothing can be loved apart from that through which whatever exists has its existence. Either take away nativity, and then show us your man; or else withdraw the flesh, and then present to our view the being whom God has redeemed—since it is these very conditions(12) which constitute the man whom God has redeemed. And are you for turning these conditions into occasions of blushing to the very creature whom He has redeemed, (censuring them), too, us unworthy of Him who certainly would not have redeemed them had He not loved them? Our birth He reforms from death by a second birth from heaven;(13) our flesh He restores from every harassing malady; when leprous, He cleanses it of the stain; when blind, He rekindles its light; when palsied, He renews its strength; when possessed with devils, He exorcises it; when dead, He reanimates it,—then shall we blush to own it? If, to be sure,(14) He had chosen to be born of a mere animal, and were to preach the kingdom of heaven invested with the body of a beast either wild or tame, your censure (I imagine) would have instantly met Him with this demurrer: "This is disgraceful for God, and 'this is unworthy of the Son of God, and simply foolish." For no other reason than because one thus judges. It is of course foolish, if we are to judge God by our own conceptions. But, Marcion, consider well this Scripture, if indeed you have not erased it: "God hath chosen the foolish things of the world, to confound the wise."(15) Now what are those foolish things? Are they the conversion of men to the worship of the true God, the rejection of error, the whole training in righteousness, chastity, mercy, patience, and innocence? These things certainly are not "foolish." Inquire again, then, of what things he spoke, and when you imagine that you have discovered what they are will you find anything to be so "foolish" as believing in a God that has been born, and that of a virgin, and of a fleshly nature too, who wallowed in all the before–mentioned humiliations of nature? But some one may say, "These are not the foolish things; they must be other things which God has chosen to confound the wisdom of the world." And yet, according to the world's wisdom, it is more easy to believe that Jupiter became a bull or a swan, if we listen to Marcion, than that Christ really became a man.

CHAP. V.—CHRIST TRULY LIVED AND DIED IN HUMAN FLESH. INCIDENTS OF HIS HUMAN LIFE ON EARTH, AND REFUTATION OF MARCION'S DOCETIC PARODY OF THE SAME.

There are, to be sure, other things also quite as foolish (as the birth of Christ), which have reference to the humiliations and sufferings of God. Or else, let them call a crucified God "wisdom." But Marcion will apply the knife' to this doctrine also,, and even with greater reason. For which Is more unworthy of God, which is more likely to raise a blush of shame, that God should be born, or that He should die? that He should bear the flesh, or the cross? be circumcised, or be crucified? be cradled, or be coffined?(2) be laid in a manger, or in a tomb? Talk of "wisdom!" You will show more of fiat if you refuse to believe this also. But, after all, you will not be "wise" unless you become a "fool" to the world, by believing" the foolish things of God." Have you, then, cut away(3) all sufferings from Christ, on the ground that, as a mere phantom, He was incapable of experiencing them? We have said above that He might possibly have undergone the unreal mockeries(4) of an imaginary birth and infancy. But answer me at once, you that murder truth: Was not God really crucified? And, having been really crucified, did He not really die? And, having indeed really died, did He not really rise again? Falsely did Paul(5) "determine to know nothing amongst us but Jesus and Him crucified;"(6) falsely has he impressed upon us that He was buried; falsely inculcated that He rose again. False, therefore, is our faith also. And all that we hope for from Christ will be a phantom. O thou most infamous of men, who acquittest of all guilt(7) the murderers of God! For nothing did Christ suffer from them, if He really suffered nothing at all. Spare the whole world's one only hope, thou who art destroying the indispensable dishonour of our faith? Whatsoever is unworthy of God, is gain to me. I am safe, if I am not ashamed—my Lord. "Whosoever," says He, "shall be ashamed of me, of him will I also be ashamed."(9) Other matters for shame find I r none which can prove me to be shameless t in a good sense, and foolish in a happy one, by my own contempt of shame. The Son of God was crucified; I am not ashamed because men must needs be ashamed of it. And the Son of God died; it is by all means to be believed, because it is absurd.(10) And He was buried, and rose again; the fact is certain, because it is impossible. But how will all this be true in Him, if He was not Himself true—if He really had not in Himself that which might be crucified, might die, might be buried, and might rise again? I mean this flesh suffused with blood, built up with bones, interwoven with nerves, entwined with veins, a flesh which knew how to be born, and how to die, human without doubt, as born of a human being. It will therefore be mortal in Christ, because Christ is man and the Son of man. Else why is Christ man and the Son of man, if he has nothing of man, and nothing from man? Unless it be either that man is anything else than flesh, or man's flesh comes from any other source than man, or Mary is anything else than a human being, or Marcion's man is as Marcion's god.(11) Otherwise Christ could not be described as being man without flesh, nor the Son of man without any human parent; just as He is not God without the Spirit of God, nor the Son of God without having God for His father. Thus the nature(12) of the two substances displayed Him as man and God,—in one respect born, in the other unborn; l in one respect fleshly in the other spiritual; in one sense weak in the other exceeding strong; in on sense dying, in the other living. This property of the two states—the divine and the human—is distinctly asserted(13) with equal truth of both natures alike, with the same belief both in respect of the Spirit '* and of the flesh. The powers of the Spirit,(14) proved Him to be God, His sufferings attested the flesh of man. If His powers were not without the Spirit(14) in like manner, were not His sufferings without the flesh. if His flesh with .its sufferings was fictitious, for the same reason was the Spirit false with all its powers. Wherefore halve(15) Christ with a lie? He was wholly the truth. Believe me, He chose rather to be born, than in any part to pretend—and that indeed to His own detriment—that He was bearing about a flesh hardened without bones, solid without muscles, bloody without blood, clothed without the tunic of skin,(1) hungry without appetite, eating without teeth, speaking without a tongue, so that His word was a phantom to the ears through an imaginary voice. A phantom, too, it was of course after the resurrection, when, showing His hands and His feet for the disciples to examine, He said, "Behold and see that it is I myself, for a spirit hath not flesh and bones, as ye see me have;"(2) without doubt, hands, and feet, and bones are not what a spirit possesses, but only the flesh. How do you interpret this statement, Marcion, you who tell us that Jesus comes only from the most excellent God, who is both simple and good? See how He rather cheats, and deceives, and juggles the eyes of all, and the senses of all, as well as their access to and contact with Him! You ought rather to have brought Christ down, not from heaven, but from some troop of mountebanks, not as God besides man, but simply as a man, a magician; not as the High Priest of our salvation, but as the conjurer in a show; not as the raiser of the dead, but as the misleader(3) of the living,—except that, if He were a magician, He must have had a nativity!

CHAP. VI.—THE DOCTRINE OF APELLES REFUTED, THAT CHRIST'S BODY WAS OF SIDEREAL SUBSTANCE, NOT BORN. NATIVITY AND MORTALITY ARE CORRELATIVE CIRCUMSTANCES, AND IN CHRIST'S CASE HIS DEATH PROVES HIS BIRTH.

But certain disciples 4 of the heretic of Pontus, compelled to be wiser than their teacher, concede to Christ real flesh, without effect, however, on(5) their denial of His nativity. He might have had, they say, a flesh which was not at all born. So we have found our way "out of a frying–pan," as the proverb runs, "into the fire,"(6)—from Marcion to Apelles. This man having first fallen from the principles of Marcion into (intercourse with) a woman, in the flesh, and afterwards shipwrecked himself, in the spirit, on the virgin Philumene,(7) proceeded from that time(8) to preach that the body of Christ was of solid flesh, but without having been born. To this angel, indeed, of Philumene, the apostle will reply in tones like those in which he even then predicted him, saying, "Although an angel from heaven preach any other gospel unto you than that which we have preached unto you, let him be accursed."(9) To the arguments, however, which have been indicated just above, we have now to show our resistance. They allow that Christ really had a body. Whence was the material of it, if not from the same sort of thing as(10) that in which He appeared? Whence came His body, if His body were not flesh? Whence came His flesh, if it were not born? Inasmuch as that which is born must undergo this nativity in order to

13

become flesh. He borrowed, they say, His flesh from the stars, and from the substances of the higher world. And they assert it for a certain principle, that a body without nativity is nothing to be astonished at, because it has been submitted to angels to appear even amongst ourselves in the flesh without the intervention of the womb. We admit, of course, that such facts have been related. But then, how comes it to pass that a faith which holds to a different rule borrows materials for its own arguments from the faith which it impugns? What has it to do with Moses, who has rejected the God of Moses? Since the God is a different one, everything belonging to him must be different also. But let the heretics always use the Scriptures of that God whose world they also enjoy. The fact will certainly recoil on them as a witness to judge them, that they maintain their own blasphemies from examples derived from Him.(11) But it is an easy task for the truth to prevail without raising any such demurrer against them. When, therefore, they set forth the flesh of Christ after the pattern of the angels, declaring it to be not born, and yet flesh for all that, I should wish them to compare the causes, both in Christ's case and that of the angels, wherefore they came in the flesh. Never did any angel descend for the purpose of being crucified, of tasting death, and of rising again from the dead. Now, since there never was such a reason for angels becoming embodied, you have the cause why they assumed flesh without undergoing birth. They had not come to die, therefore they also (came not) to be born. Christ, however, having been sent to die, had necessarily to be also born, that He might be capable of death; for nothing is in the habit of dying but that which is born. Between nativity and mortality there is a mutual contrast. The law(1) which makes us die is the cause of our being born. Now, since Christ died owing to the condition which undergoes death, but that undergoes death which is also born, the consequence was—nay,it was an antecedent necessity–that He must have been born also,(2) by reason of the condition which undergoes birth; because He had to die in obedience to that very condition which, because it begins with birth, ends in death.(3) It was not fitting for Him not to be born under the pretence (4) that it was fitting for Him to die. But the Lord Himself at that very time appeared to Abraham amongst those angels without being born, and yet in the flesh without doubt, in virtue of the before–mentioned diversity of cause. You, however, cannot admit this, since you do not receive that Christ, who was even then rehearsing(5) how to converse with, and liberate, and judge the human race, in the habit of a flesh which as yet was not born, because it did not yet mean to die until both its nativity and mortality were previously (by

14

prophecy) announced. Let them, then, prove to us that those angels derived their flesh from the stars. If they do not prove it because it is not written, neither will the flesh of Christ get its origin therefrom, for which they borrowed the precedent of the angels. It is plain that the angels bore a flesh which was not naturally their own; their nature being of a spiritual substance, although in some sense peculiar to themselves, corporeal; and yet they could be transfigured into human shape, and for the time be able to appear and have intercourse with men. Since, therefore, it has not been told us whence they obtained their flesh, it remains for us not to doubt in our minds that a property of angelic power is this, to assume to themselves bodily Shape out of no material substance. How much more, you say, is it (within their competence to take a body) out of some material substance? That is true enough. But there is no evidence of this, because Scripture says nothing. Then, again,(6) how should they who are able to form themselves into that which by nature they are not, be unable to do this out of no material substance? If they become that which they are not, why cannot they so become out of that which is not? But that which has not existence when it comes into existence, is made out of nothing. This is why it is unnecessary either to inquire or to demonstrate what has subsequently become of their (7) bodies. What came out of nothing, came to nothing. They, who were able to convert themselves into flesh have it in their power to convert nothing itself into flesh. It is a greater thing to change a nature than to make matter. But even if it were necessary to suppose that angels derived their flesh from some material substance, it is surely more credible that it was from some earthly matter than from any kind of celestial substances, since it was composed of so palpably terrene a quality that it fed on earthly ailments. Suppose that even now a celestial flesh (8) had fed on earthly aliments, although it was not itself earthly, in the same way that earthly flesh actually fed on celestial aliments, although it had nothing of the celestial nature (for we read of manna having been food for the people: "Man," says the Psalmist, "did eat angels' bread,"(9)) yet this does not once infringe the separate condition of the Lord's flesh, because of His different destination. For One who was to be truly a man, even unto death, it was necessary that He should be clothed with that flesh to which death belongs. Now that flesh to which death belongs is preceded by birth.

CHAP. VII.—EXPLANATION OF THE LORD'S QUESTION ABOUT HIS MOTHER AND HIS BRETHREN. ANSWER TO THE CAVILS OF APELLES AND MARCION, WHO SUPPORT THEIR DENIAL OF CHRIST'S NATIVITY BY IT.

But whenever a dispute arises about the nativity, all who reject it as creating a presumption in favour of the reality of Christ's flesh, wilfully deny that God Himself was born, on the ground that He asked, "Who is my mother, and who are my brethren? " (10) Let, therefore, Apelles hear what was our answer to Marcion in that little work, in which we challenged his own (favourite) gospel to the proof, even that the material circumstances of that remark (of the Lord's) should be considered.(11) First of all, nobody would have told Him that His mother and brethren were standing outside, if he were not certain both that He had a mother and brethren, and that they were the very persons whom he was then announcing,—who had either been known to him before, or were then and there discovered by him; although heretics(12) have removed this passage from the gospel, because those who were admiring His doctrine said that His supposed father, Joseph the carpenter, and His mother Mary, and His brethren, and His sisters, were very well known to them. But it was with the view of tempting Him, that they had mentioned to Him a mother and brethren which He did not possess. The Scripture says nothing of this, although it is not in other instances silent when anything was done against Him by way of temptation. "Behold," it says, "a certain lawyer stood up, and tempted Him." (1) And in another passage: "The Pharisees also came unto Him, tempting Him." Who (2) was to prevent its being in this place also indicated that this was done with the view of tempting Him? I do not admit what you advance of your own apart from Scripture. Then there ought to be suggested s some occasion (4) for the temptation. What could they have thought to be in Him which required temptation? The question, to be sure, whether He had been born or not? For if this point were denied in His answer, it might come out on the announcement of a temptation. And yet no temptation, when aiming at the discovery of the point which prompts the temptation by its doubtfulness, falls upon one so abruptly, as not to be preceded by the question

16

which compels the temptation whilst raising the doubt. Now, since the nativity of Christ had never come into question, how can you contend that they meant by their temptation to inquire about a point on which they had never raised a doubt? Besides,(5) if He had to be tempted about His birth, this of course was not the proper way of doing it,—by announcing those persons who, even on the supposition of His birth, might possibly not have been in existence. We have all been born, and yet all of us have not either brothers or mother. He might with more probability have had even a father than a mother, and uncles more likely than brothers. Thus is the temptation about His birth unsuitable, for it might have been contrived without any mention of either His mother or His brethren. It is clearly more credible that, being certain that He had both a mother and brothers, they tested His divinity rather than His nativity, whether, when within, He knew what was without; being tried by the untrue announcement of the presence of persons who were not present. But the artifice of a temptation might have been thwarted thus: it might have happened that He knew that those whom they were announcing to be "standing without," were in fact absent by the stress either of sickness, or of business, or a journey which He was at the time aware of. No one tempts (another) in a way in which he knows that he may have himself to bear the shame of the temptation. There being, then, no suitable occasion for a temptation, the announcement that His mother and His brethren had actually turned up(6) recovers its naturalness. But there is some ground for thinking that Christ's answer denies His mother and brethren for the present, as even Apelles might learn. "The Lord's brethren had not yet believed in Him." (7) So is it contained in the Gospel which was published before Marcion's time; whilst there is at the same time a want of evidence of His mother's adherence to Him, although the Marthas and the other Marys were in constant attendance on Him. In this very passage indeed, their unbelief is evident. Jesus was teaching the way of life, preaching the kingdom of God and actively engaged in healing infirmities of body and soul; but all the while, whilst strangers were intent on Him, His very nearest relatives were absent. By and by they turn up, and keep outside; but they do not go in, because, forsooth, they set small store(8) on that which was doing within; nor do they even wait,(9) as if they had something which they could contribute more necessary than that which He was so earnestly doing; but they prefer to interrupt Him, and wish to call Him away from His great work Now, I ask you, Apelles, or will you Marcion, please (to tell me), if you happened to be at a stage play, or had laid a wager (10) on a foot race or a chariot race, and were called away by such a message, would you not have exclaimed, "What are mother and brothers to me?" (11) And did not Christ, whilst preaching and manifesting God, fulfilling the law and the prophets, and scattering the darkness of the long preceding age, justly employ this same form of words, in order to strike the unbelief of those who stood outside, or to shake off the importunity of those who would call Him away from His work? If, however, He had meant to deny His own nativity, He would have found place, time, and means for expressing Himself very differently,(12) and not in words which might be uttered by one who had both a mother and brothers. When denying one's parents in indignation, one does not deny their existence, but censures their faults. Besides, He gave Others the preference; and since He shows their title to this favour—even because they listened to the word (of God)—He points out in what sense He denied His mother and His brethren. For in whatever sense He adopted as His own those who adhered to Him, in that' did He deny as His· those who kept aloof from Him. Christ also is wont to do to the utmost that which He enjoins on others. How strange, then, would it certainly(2) have been, if, while he was teaching others not to esteem mother, or father, or brothers, as highly as the word of God, He were Himself to leave the word of God as soon as His mother and brethren were announced to Him! He denied His parents, then, in the sense in which He has taught us to deny ours—for God's work. But there is also another view of the case: in the abjured mother there is a figure of the synagogue, as well as of the Jews in the unbelieving brethren. In their person Israel remained outside, whilst the new disciples who kept close to Christ within, hearing and believing, represented the Church, which He called mother in a preferable sense and a worthier brotherhood, with the repudiation of the carnal relationship. It was in just the same sense, indeed, that He also replied to that exclamation (of a certain woman), not denying His mother's "womb and paps," but designating those as more "blessed who hear the word of God." (3)

CHAP. VIII.—APELLES AND HIS FOLLOWERS, DISPLEASED WITH OUR EARTHLY BODIES, ATTRIBUTED TO CHRIST A BODY OF A PURER SORT. HOW CHRIST WAS HEAVENLY EVEN IN HIS EARTHLY FLESH.

ON THE FLESH OF CHRIST

These passages alone, in which Apelles and Marcion seem to place their chief reliance when interpreted according to the truth of the entire uncorrupted gospel, ought to have been sufficient for proving the human flesh of Christ by a defence of His birth. But since Apelles' precious set (4) lay a very great stress on the shameful condition s of the flesh, which they will have to have been furnished with souls tampered with by the fiery author of evil,(6) and so unworthy of Christ; and because they on that account suppose that a sidereal substance is suitable for Him, I am bound to refute them on their own ground. They mention a certain angel of great renown as having created this world of ours, and as having, after the creation, repented of his work. This indeed we have treated of in a passage by itself; for we have written a little work in opposition to them, on the question whether one who had the spirit, and will, and power of Christ for such operations, could have done anything which required repentance, since they describe the said angel by the figure of "the lost sheep." The world, then, must be a wrong thing,(7) according to the evidence of its Creator's repentance; for all repentance is the admission of fault, nor has it indeed any existence except through fault. Now, if the world (8) is a fault, as is the body, such must be its parts—faulty too; so in like manner must be the heaven and its celestial (contents), and everything which is conceived and produced out of it. And "a corrupt tree must needs bring forth evil fruit." (9) The flesh of Christ, therefore, if composed of celestial elements, consists of faulty materials, sinful by reason of its sinful origin; (10) so that it must be a part of that substance which they disdain to clothe Christ with, because of its sinfulness,—in other words, our own. Then, as there is no difference in the point of ignominy, let them either devise for Christ some substance of a purer stamp, since they are displeased with our own, or else let them recognise this too, than which even a heavenly substance could not have been better. We read in so many words:(11)"The first man is of the earth, earthy; the second man is the Lord from heaven."(12) This passage, however, has nothing to do with any difference of substance; it only contrasts with the once (13) "earthy" substance of the flesh of the first man, Adam, the "heavenly" substance of the spirit of the second man, Christ. And so entirely does the passage refer the celestial man to the spirit and not to the flesh, that those whom it compares to Him evidently become celestial—by the Spirit, of course—even in this "earthy flesh." Now, since Christ is heavenly even in regard to the flesh, they could not be compared to Him, who are not heavenly in reference to their flesh.(14) If, then, they who become heavenly, as Christ also was, carry about an "earthy" substance of flesh, the conclusion which is affirmed by this fact is, that Christ Himself also was heavenly, but in an "earthy" flesh, even as they are who are put on a level with Him.(15)

CHAP. IX.—CHRIST'S FLESH PERFECTLY NATURAL, LIKE OUR OWN. NONE OF THE SUPERNATURAL FEATURES WHICH THE HERETICS ASCRIBED TO IT DISCOVERABLE, ON A CAREFUL VIEW.

We have thus far gone on the principle, that nothing which is derived from some other thing, however different it may be from that from which it is derived, is so different as not to suggest the source from which it comes. No material substance is without the witness of its own original, however great a change into new properties it may have undergone. There is this very body of ours, the formation of which out of the dust of the ground is a truth which has found its way into Gentile fables; it certainly testifies its own origin from the two elements of earth and water,—from the former by its flesh, from the latter by its blood. Now, although there is a difference in the appearance of qualities (in other words,that which proceeds from something else is in development (1) different), yet, after all, what is blood but red fluid? what is flesh but earth in an especial (2) form? Consider the respective qualities,—of the muscles as clods; of the bones as stones; the mamillary glands as a kind of pebbles. Look upon the close junctions of the nerves as propagations of roots, and the branching courses of the veins as winding rivulets, and the down (which covers us) as moss, and the hair as grass, and the very treasures of marrow within our bones as ores, of flesh. All these marks of the earthy origin were in Christ; and it is they which obscured Him as the Son of God, for He was looked on as man, for no other reason whatever than because He existed in the corporeal substance of a man. Or else, show us some celestial substance in Him purloined from the Bear, and the Pleiades, and the Hyades. Well, then, the characteristics which we have enumerated are so many proofs that His was an earthy flesh, as ours is; but anything new or anything strange I do not discover. Indeed it was from His words and actions only, from His teaching and miracles solely, that men, though amazed, owned Christ to be

20

man.(4) But if there had been in Him any new kind of flesh miraculously obtained (from the stars), it would have been certainly well known.s As the case stood, however, it was actually the ordinary(6) condition of His terrene flesh which made all things else about Him wonderful, as when they said, "Whence hath this man this wisdom and these mighty works?"(7) Thus spake even they who despised His outward form. His body did not reach even to human beauty, to say nothing of heavenly glory.(8) Had the prophets given us no information whatever concerning His ignoble appearance, His very sufferings and the very contumely He endured bespeak it all. The sufferings attested His human flesh, the contumely proved its abject condition. Would any man have dared to touch even with his little finger, the body of Christ, if it had been of an unusual nature;, or to smear His face with spitting, if it had not invited it (10) (by its abjectness)? Why talk of a heavenly flesh, when you have no grounds to offer us for your celestial theory?(10) Why deny it to be earthy, when you have the best of reasons for knowing it to be earthy? He hungered under the devil's temptation; He thirsted with the woman of Samaria; He wept over Lazarus; He trembles at death (for "the flesh," as He says, "is weak "(12)); at last, He pours out His blood. These, I suppose, are celestial marks? But how, I ask, could He have incurred contempt and suffering in the way I have described, if there had beamed forth in that flesh of His aught of celestial excellence? From this, therefore, we have a convincing proof that in it there was nothing of heaven, because it must be capable of contempt and suffering.

CHAP. X.—ANOTHER CLASS OF HERETICS REFUTED. THEY ALLEGED THAT CHRIST'S FLESH WAS OF A FINER TEXTURE, ANIMALIS, COMPOSED OF SOUL.

I now turn to another class, who are equally wise in their own conceit. They affirm that the flesh of Christ is composed of soul,(13) that His soul became flesh, so that His flesh is soul; and as His flesh is of soul, so is His soul of flesh. But here, again, I must have some reasons. If, in order to save the soul, Christ took a soul within Himself, because it could not be saved except by Him having, it within Himself, I see no reason why, in clothing Himself with flesh, He should have made that flesh one of soul,(14) as if He could not have saved the soul in any other way than by making flesh of it. For while He saves our souls, which are not only not of flesh,(15) but are even distinct from flesh, how much more able was He to secure salvation to that soul which He took Himself, when it was also not of flesh? Again, since they assume it as a main tenet,(1) that Christ came forth not to deliver the flesh, but only our soul, how absurd it is, in the first place, that, meaning to save only the soul, He yet made it into just that sort of bodily substance which He had no intention of saving! And, secondly, if He had undertaken deliver our souls by means of that which He carried, He ought, in that soul which He carried to have carried our soul, one (that is) of the same condition as ours; and whatever is the condition of our soul in its secret nature, it is certainly not one of flesh. However, it was not our soul which He saved, if His own was of flesh; for ours is not of flesh. Now, if He did not save our soul on the ground, that it was a soul of flesh which He saved, He is nothing to us, because He has not saved our soul. Nor indeed did it need salvation, for it was not our soul really, since it was, on the supposition,(2) a soul of flesh. But yet it is evident that it has been saved. Of flesh, therefore, it was not composed, and it was ours; for it was our soul that was saved, since that was in peril of damnation. We therefore now conclude that as in Christ the soul was not of flesh, so neither could His flesh have possibly been composed of soul.

CHAP. XI.—THE OPPOSITE EXTRAVAGANCE EXPOSED. THAT IS CHRIST WITH A SOUL COMPOSED OF FLESH—CORPOREAL, THOUGH INVISIBLE. CHRIST'S SOUL, LIKE OURS, DISTINCT FROM FLESH, THOUGH CLOTHED IN IT.

But we meet another argument of theirs, when we raise the question why Christ, in assuming a flesh composed of soul, should seem to have had a soul that was made of flesh? For God, they say, desired to make the soul visible to men, by enduing it with a bodily nature, although it was before invisible; of its own nature, indeed, it was incapable of seeing anything, even its own self, by reason of the obstacle of this flesh, so that it was even a matter of doubt whether it was born or not. The soul, therefore (they further say), was made corporeal in Christ, in order that we might see it when undergoing birth, and death, and (what is more) resurrection. But yet, how was this possible, that by means of the flesh the soul should demonstrate itself(3) to itself or to us, when it could not possibly be ascertained that it would offer this mode of exhibiting itself by the flesh, until the thing came into existence to which it was unknown,(4) that is to say, the flesh? It received darkness, forsooth, in order to be able to shine! Now,(5) let us first turn our attention to this point, whether it was requisite that the soul should exhibit itself in the manner contended for;(5) and next consider whether their previous position be (7) that the soul is wholly invisible(inquiring further) whether this invisibility is the result of its incorporeality, or whether it actually possesses some sort of body peculiar to itself. And yet, although they say that it is invisible, they determine it to be corporeal, but having somewhat that is invisible. For if it has nothing invisible how can it be said to be invisible? But even its existence is an impossibility, unless it has that which is instrumental to its existence.(8) Since, however, it exists, it must needs have a something through which it exists. If it has this something, it must be its body. Everything which exists is r a bodily existence sui generis. Nothing lacks bodily existence but that which is non-existent. If, then, the soul has an invisible body, He who had proposed to make it(9) visible would certainly have done His work better (10) if He had made that part of it which was accounted invisible, visible; because then there would have been no untruth or weakness in the case, and neither of these flaws is suitable to God. (But as the case stands in the hypothesis) there is untruth, since He has set forth the soul as being a different thing from what it really is; and there is weakness, since He was unable to make it appear (11) to be that which it is. No one who wishes to exhibit a man covers him with a veil (12) or a mask. This, however, is precisely what has been done to the soul, if it has been clothed with a covering belonging to something else, by being converted into flesh. But even if the soul is, on their hypothesis, supposed (13) to be incorporeal, so that the soul, whatever it is, should by some mysterious force of the reason (14) be quite unknown, only not be a body, then in that case it were not beyond the power of God—indeed it would be more consistent with His plan—if He displayed (15) the soul in some new sort of body, different from that which we all have in common, one of which we should have quite a different notion,(16) (being spared the idea that)(1) He had set His mind on(2) making, without an adequate cause, a visible soul instead of (3) an invisible one—a fit incentive, no doubt, for such questions as they start,(4) by their maintenance of a human flesh for it.(5) Christ, however, could not have appeared among men except as a man. Restore, therefore, to Christ, His faith; believe that He who willed to walk the earth as a man exhibited even a soul of a thoroughly human condition, not making it of flesh, but clothing it with flesh.

CHAP. XII.—THE TRUE FUNCTIONS OF THE SOUL. CHRIST ASSUMED IT IN HIS PERFECT HUMAN NATURE, NOT TO REVEAL AND EXPLAIN IT, BUT TO SAVE IT. ITS RESURRECTION WITH THE BODY ASSURED BY CHRIST.

Well, now, let it be granted that the soul is made apparent by the flesh,(6) on the assumption that it was evidently necessary (7) that it should be made apparent in some way or other, that is, as being incognizable to itself and to us: there is still an absurd distinction in this hypothesis, which implies that we are ourselves separate from our soul, when all that we are is soul. Indeed,(8) without the soul we are nothing; there is not even the name of a human being, only that of a carcase. If, then, we are ignorant of the soul, it is in fact the soul that is ignorant of itself. Thus the only remaining question left for us to look into is, whether the soul was in this matter so ignorant of itself that it became known in any way it could.(9) The soul, in my opinion,(10) is sensual.(11) Nothing, therefore, pertaining to the soul is unconnected with sense,(12) nothing pertaining to sense is unconnected with the soul.(13) And if I may use the expression for the sake of emphasis, I would say, "Animae anima sensus est"—"Sense is the soul's very soul." Now, since it is the soul that imparts the faculty of perception(14) to all (that have sense), and since it is itself that perceives the very senses, not to say properties, of them all how is it likely that it did not itself receive sense as its own natural constitution? Whence is it to know what is necessary for itself under given circumstances, from the very necessity of natural causes, if it knows not its own property, and what is necessary for it? To recognise this indeed is within the competence of every soul; it has, I mean, a practical knowledge of itself, without which knowledge of itself no soul could possibly have exercised its own functions.(15) I suppose, too, that it is especially suitable that man, the only rational animal, should have been furnished with such a soul as would make him the rational animal, itself being pre—eminently rational. Now, how can that soul which makes man a rational animal be itself rational if it be itself ignorant of its rationality, being ignorant of its own very self? So far, however, is it from being ignorant, that it knows its own Author, its own Master, and its own condition. Before it learns anything about God, it names the name of God. Before it acquires any knowledge of His judgment, it professes to commend itself to God. There is nothing one oftener hears of than that there is rio hope after death; and yet what imprecations or deprecations does not the soul use according as the man dies after a well or ill spent life! These reflections are more fully pursued in a short treatise which we have written, "On the Testimony of the Soul." (16) Besides, if the soul was ignorant of itself from the beginning, there is nothing it could (17) have learnt of Christ except its own quality.(18) It was not its own form that it learnt of Christ, but its salvation. For this cause did the Son of God descend and take on Him a soul, not that the soul might discover itself in Christ, but Christ in itself. For its salvation is endangered, not by its being ignorant of itself, but of the word of God. "The life," says He, "was manifested," (19) not the soul. And again, "I am come to save the soul. He did not say, "to explain" (20) it. We could not know, of course,(21) that the soul, although an invisible essence, is born and dies, unless it were exhibited corporeally. We certainly were ignorant that it was to rise again with the flesh. This is the truth which it will be found was manifested by Christ. But even this He did not manifest in Himself in a different way than in some Lazarus, whose flesh was no more composed of soul (22) than his soul was of flesh.(23) What further knowledge, therefore, have we received of the structure (24) of the soul which we were ignorant of before? What invisible part was there belonging to it which wanted to be made visible by the flesh?

533

CHAP. XIII."—CHRIST'S HUMAN NATURE. THE FLESH AND THE SOUL BOTH FULLY AND UN—CONFUSEDLY CONTAINED IN IT.

ON THE FLESH OF CHRIST

The soul became flesh that the soul might become visible.(1) Well, then, did the flesh likewise become soul that the flesh might be manifested?(2) If the soul is flesh, it is no longer soul, but flesh. If the flesh is soul, it is no longer flesh, but soul. Where, then, there is flesh, and where there is soul, it has become both one and the other.(3) Now, if they are neither in particular, although they become both one and the other, it is, to say the least, very absurd, that we should understand the soul when we name the flesh, and when we indicate the soul, explain ourselves as meaning the flesh. All things will be in danger of being taken in a sense different from their own proper sense, and, whilst taken in that different sense, of losing their proper one, if they are called by a name which differs from their natural designation. Fidelity in names secures the safe appreciation of properties. When these properties undergo a change, they are considered to possess such qualities as their names indicate. Baked clay, for instance, receives the name of brick.(4) It retains not the name which designated its former state,(5) because it has no longer a share in that state. Therefore, also, the soul of Christ having become flesh,(6) cannot be anything else than that which it has become nor can it be any longer that which it once was, having become indeed(7) something else. And since we have just had recourse to an illustration, we will put it to further use. Our pitcher, then, which was formed of the clay, is one body, and has one name indicative, of course, of that one body; nor can the pitcher be also called clay, because what it once was, it is no longer. Now that which is no longer (what it was) is also not an inseparable property.(8) And the soul is not an inseparable property. Since, therefore, it has become flesh, the soul is a uniform solid body; it is also a wholly incomplex being,(9) and an indivisible substance. But in Christ we find the soul and the flesh expressed in simple un−figurative(10) terms; that is to say, the soul is called soul, and the flesh, flesh; nowhere is the soul termed flesh, or the flesh, soul; and yet they ought to have been thus (confusedly) named if such had been their condition. The fact, however, is that even by Christ Himself each substance has been separately mentioned by itself, conformably of course, to the distinction which exists between the properties of both, the soul by itself, and the flesh by itself." "My soul," says He, "is exceeding sorrowful, even unto death;"(11) and "the bread that I will give is my flesh, (which I will give) for the life(12) of the world.(13) Now, if the soul had been flesh, there would have only been in Christ the soul composed of flesh, or else the flesh composed of soul.(14) Since, however, He keeps the species distinct, the flesh and the soul, He shows them to be two. If two, then they are no longer one; if not one, then the soul is not composed of flesh, nor the flesh of soul. For the soul–flesh, or the flesh–soul, is but one; unless indeed He even had some other soul apart from that which was flesh, and bare about another flesh besides that which was soul. But since He had but one flesh and one soul,—that "soul which was sorrowful, even unto death," and that flesh which was the "bread given for the life of the world,"—the number is unimpaired(15) of two substances distinct in kind, thus excluding the unique species of the flesh–comprised soul.

CHAP. XIV.—CHRIST TOOK NOT ON HIM AN ANGELIC NATURE, BUT THE HUMAN. IT WAS MEN, NOT ANGELS, WHOM HE CAME TO SAVE.

But Christ, they say, bare(16) (the nature of) an angel. For what reason? The same which induced Him to become man? Christ, then, was actuated by the motive which led Him to take human nature. Man's salvation was the motive, the restoration of that which had perished. Man had perished; his recovery had become necessary. No such cause, however, existed for Christ's taking on Him the nature of angels. For although there is assigned to angels also perdition in "the fire prepared for the devil and his angels,"(17) yet a restoration is never promised to them. No charge about the salvation of angels did Christ ever receive from the Father; and that which the Father neither promised nor commanded, Christ could not have undertaken. For what object, therefore, did He bear the angelic nature, if it were not (that He might have it) as a powerful helper(18) wherewithal to execute the salvation of man? The Son of God, in sooth, was not competent alone to deliver man, whom a solitary and single serpent had overthrown! There is, then, no longer but one God, but one Saviour, if there be two to contrive salvation, and one of them in need of the other. But was it His object indeed to deliver man by an angel? Why, then, come down to do that which He was about to expedite with an angel's help? If by an angel's aid, why come Himself also? If He meant to do all by Himself, why have an angel too? He has been, it is true, called "the Angel of great counsel," that is, a messenger, by a term expressive of official function, not of nature. For He had to announce to the world the mighty purpose of the Father, even that which ordained the restoration of man. But He is not on this account to be regarded as an angel, as a Gabriel or a Michael. For the Lord of the Vineyard sends even His Son to the labourers require fruit, as well as His servants. Yet the Son will not therefore be counted as one of the servants because He undertook the office of a servant. I may, then, more easily say, if such an expression is to be hazarded,(1) that the Son is actually an angel, that is, a messenger, from the Father, than that there is an angel in the Son. Forasmuch, however, as it has been declared concerning the Son Himself, Thou hast made Him a little lower than the angels"(2) how will it appear that He put on the nature of angels if He was made lower than the angels, having become man, with flesh and soul as the Son of man? As "the Spirit(3) of God." however, and "the Power of the Highest," can He be regarded as lower than the angels,—He who is verily God, and the Son of God? Well, but as bearing human nature, He is so far made inferior to the angels; but as bearing angelic nature, He to the same degree loses that inferiority. This opinion will be very suitable for Ebion,(5) who holds Jesus to be a mere man, and nothing more than a descendant of David, and not also the Son of God; although He is, to be sure,(6) in one respect more glorious than the prophets, inasmuch as he declares that there was an angel in Him, just as there was in Zechariah. Only it was never said by Christ, "And the angel, which spake within me, said unto me."(7) Neither, indeed, was ever used by Christ that familiar phrase of all the prophets, "Thus saith the Lord." For He was Himself the Lord, who openly spake by His own authority, prefacing His words with the formula, "Verily, verily, I say unto you." What need is there of further argument? Hear what Isaiah says in emphatic words, "It was no angel, nor deputy, but the Lord Himself who saved them."(8)

CHAP. XV.—THE VALENTINIAN FIGMENT OF CHRIST'S FLESH BEING OF A SPIRITUAL NATURE, EXAMINED AND REFUTED OUT OF SCRIPTURE.

Valentinus, indeed, on the strength of his heretical system, might consistently devise a spiritual flesh for Christ. Any one who refused to believe that that flesh was human might pretend it to be anything he liked, for—as much as (and this remark is applicable, to all heretics), if it was not human, and was not born of man, I do not see of what substance Christ Himself spoke when He called Himself man and the Son of man, saying: "But now ye seek to kill me, a man that hath told you the truth;"(9) and "The Son of man is Lord of the Sabbath–day."(10 For it is of Him that Isaiah writes: "A man of suffering, and acquainted with the bearing of weakness;"(11) and Jeremiah: "He is a man, and who hath known Him?"(12) and Daniel: "Upon the clouds (He came) as the Son of man."(13) The Apostle Paul likewise says: "The man Christ Jesus is the one Mediator between God and man."(14) Also Peter, in the Acts of the Apostles, speaks of Him as verily human (when he says), "Jesus Christ was a man approved of God among you."(15) These passages alone ought to suffice as a prescriptive(16) testimony in proof that Christ had human flesh derived from man, and not spiritual, and that His flesh was not composed. of soul,(17) nor of stellar substance, and that it was not an imaginary flesh; (and no doubt they would be sufficient) if heretics could only divest themselves of all their contentious warmth and artifice. For, as I have read in some writer of Valentinus' wretched faction,(18) they refuse at the outset to believe that a human and earthly substance was created(19) for Christ, lest the Lord should be regarded as inferior to the angels, who are not formed of earthly flesh; whence, too, it would be necessary that, if His flesh were like ours, it should be similarly born, not of the Spirit, nor of God, but of the will of man. Why, moreover, should it be born, not of corruptible [seed], but of incorruptible? Why, again, since His flesh has both risen and returned to heaven, is not ours, being like His, also taken up at once? Or else, why does not His flesh, since it is like ours, return in like manner to the ground, and suffer dissolution? Such objections even the heathen used constantly to bandy about.(1) Was the Son of God reduced to such a depth of degradation Again, if He rose again as a precedent for our hope, how is it that nothing like it has been thought desirable (to happen) to ourselves? Such views are not improper for heathens and they are fit and natural for the heretics too. For, indeed, what difference is there between them, except it be that the heathen, in not believing, do believe; while the heretics, in believing, do not believe? Then, again, they read: "Thou madest Him a little less than angels;"(3) and they deny the lower nature of that Christ who declares Himself to be, "not a man, but a worm;"(4) who also had "no form nor comeliness, but His form was ignoble, despised more than all men, a man in suffering, and acquainted with the bearing of weakness."(5) Here they discover a human being mingled with a divine one and so they deny the manhood. They believe that He died, and maintain that a being which has died was born of an incorruptible substance;(6) as if, forsooth, corruptibility(7) were something else than death! But our flesh, too, ought immediately to have risen again. Wait a while. Christ has not yet subdued His enemies, so as to be able to triumph over them in company with His friends.

CHAP. XVI.—CHRIST'S FLESH IN NATURE, THE SAME AS OURS, ONLY SINLESS. THE DIFFERENCE BETWEEN CARNEM PECCATI AND PECCATUM CARNIS: IT IS THE LATTER WHICH CHRIST ABOLISHED. THE FLESH OF THE FIRST ADAM, NO LESS THAN THAT OF THE SECOND ADAM, NOT RECEIVED FROM HUMAN SEED, ALTHOUGH AS ENTIRELY HUMAN AS OUR OWN, WHICH IS DERIVED FROM IT.

The famous Alexander,(8) too, instigated by his love of disputation in the true fashion of heretical temper, has made himself conspicuous against us; he will have us say that Christ put on flesh of an earthly origin,(9) in order that He might in His own person abolish sinful flesh.(10) Now, even if we did assert this as our opinion, we should be able to defend it in such a way as completely to avoid the extravagant folly which he ascribes to us in making us suppose that the very flesh of Christ was in Himself abolished as being sinful; because we mention our belief (in public),(11) that it is sitting at the right hand of the Father in heaven; and we further declare that it will come again from thence in all the pomp(12) of the Father's glory: it is therefore just as impossible for us to say that it is abolished, as it is for us to maintain that it is sinful, and so made void, since in it there has been no fault. We maintain, moreover, that what has been abolished in Christ is not carnem peccati, "sinful flesh," but peccatum carnis, "sin in the flesh,"—not the material thing, but its condition;(13) not the substance, but its flaw;(14) and (this we aver) on the authority of the apostle, who says, "He abolished sin in the flesh."(15) Now in another sentence he says that Christ was "in the likeness of sinful flesh,"(16)not, however, as if He had taken on Him "the

30

likeness of the flesh," in the sense of a semblance of body instead of its reality; but he means us to understand likeness to the flesh which sinned,(17) because the flesh of Christ, which committed no sin itself, resembled that which had sinned,—resembled it in its nature, but not in the corruption it received from Adam; whence we also affirm that there was in Christ the same flesh as that whose nature in man is sinful. In the flesh, therefore, we say that sin has been abolished, because in Christ that same flesh is maintained without sin, which in than was not maintained without sin. Now, it would not contribute to the purpose of Christ's abolishing sin in the flesh, if He did not abolish it in that flesh in which was the nature of sin, nor (would it conduce) to His glory. For surely it would have been no strange thing if He had removed the stain of sin in some better flesh, and one which should possess a different, even a sinless, nature! Then, you say, if He took our flesh, Christ's was a sinful one. Do not, however, fetter with mystery a sense which is quite intelligible. For in putting on our flesh, He made it His own; in making it His own, He made it sinless. A word of caution, however, must be addressed to all who refuse to believe that our flesh was in Christ on the ground that it came not of the seed of a human father,(1) let them remember that Adam himself received this flesh of ours without the seed of a human father. As earth was converted into this flesh of ours without the seed of a human father, so also was it quite possible for the Son of God to take to Himself the substance of the selfsame flesh, without a human father's agency.(3)

CHAP, XVII.—THE SIMILARITY OF CIRCUMSTANCES BETWEEN THE FIRST AND THE SECOND ADAM, AS TO THE DERIVATION OF THEIR FLESH. AN ANALOGY ALSO PLEASANTLY TRACED BETWEEN EVE AND THE VIRGIN MARY.

But, leaving Alexander with his syllogisms, which he so perversely applies in his discussions, as well as with the hymns of Valentinus, which, with consummate assurance, he interpolates as the production of some respectable(4) author, let us confine our inquiry to a single point—Whether Christ received flesh from the virgin?—that we may thus arrive at a certain proof that His flesh was human, if He derived its substance from His mother's womb, although we are at once furnished with clear evidences of the human character of His flesh, from its name and description as that of a man, and from the nature of its constitution, and from the system of its sensations, and from its suffering of death. Now, it will first by necessary to show what previous reason there was for the Son of God's being born of a virgin. He who was going to consecrate a new order of birth, must Himself be born after a novel fashion, concerning which Isaiah foretold how that the Lord Himself would give the sign. What, then, is the sign? "Behold a virgin shall conceive and bear a son."(5) Accordingly, a virgin did conceive and bear "Emmanuel, God with us."(6) This is the new nativity; a man is born in God. And in this man God was born, taking the flesh of an ancient race, without the help, however, of the ancient seed, in order that He might reform it with a new seed, that is, in a spiritual manner, and cleanse it by the re-moral of all its ancient stains. But the whole of this new birth was prefigured, as was the case in all other instances, in ancient type, the Lord being born as man by a dispensation in which a virgin was the medium. The earth was still in a virgin state, reduced as yet by no human labour, with no seed as yet cast into its furrows, when, as we are told, God made man out of it into a living soul.(7) As, then, the first Adam is thus introduced to us, it is a just inference that the second Adam likewise, as the apostle has told us, was formed by God into a quickening spirit out of the ground,—in other words, out of a flesh which was unstained as yet by any human generation. But that I may lose no opportunity of supporting my argument from the name of Adam, why is Christ called Adam by the apostle, unless it be that, as man, He was of that earthly origin? And even reason here maintains the same conclusion, because it was by just the contrary(8) operation that God recovered His own image and likeness, of which He had been robbed by the devil. For it was while Eve was yet a virgin, that the ensnaring word had crept into her ear which was to build the edifice of death. Into a virgin's soul, in like manner, must be introduced that Word of God which was to raise the fabric of life; so that what had been reduced to ruin by this sex, might by the selfsame sex be recovered to salvation. As Eve had believed the serpent, so Mary believed the angel.(9) The delinquency which the one occasioned by believing, the other by believing effaced. But (it will be said) Eve did not at the devil's word conceive in her womb. Well, she at all events conceived; for the devil's word afterwards became as seed to her that she should conceive as an outcast, and bring forth in sorrow. Indeed she gave birth to a fratricidal devil; whilst Mary, on the contrary, bare one who was one day to secure salvation to Israel, His own brother after the flesh, and the murderer of Himself. God therefore sent down into the virgin's womb His Word, as the good Brother, who should blot out the memory of the evil brother. Hence it was necessary that Christ should come forth for the salvation of man, in that condition of flesh into which man had entered ever since his condemnation.

CHAP. XVIII.—THE MYSTERY OF THE ASSUMPTION OF OUR PERFECT HUMAN NATURE BY THE SECOND PERSON OF THE BLESSED TRINITY. HE IS HERE CALLED, AS OFTEN ELSEWHERE, THE SPIRIT.

Now, that we may give a simpler answer, it was not fit that the Son of God should be born of a human father's seed, lest, if He were wholly the Son of a man, He should fail to be also the Son of God, and have nothing more than "a Solomon" or "a Jonas,"'—as Ebion(2) thought we ought to believe concerning Him. In order, therefore, that He who was already the Son of God—of God the Father's seed, that is to say, the Spirit—might also be the Son of man, He only wanted to assume flesh, of the flesh of man(3) without the seed of a man;(4) for the seed of a man was unnecessary s for One who had the seed of God. As, then, before His birth of the virgin, He was able to have God for His Father without a human mother, so likewise, after He was born of the virgin, He was able to have a woman for His mother without a human father. He is thus man with God, in short, since He is man's flesh with God's Spirit(6)—flesh (I say) without seed from man, Spirit with seed from God. For as much, then, as the dispensation of God's purpose(7) concerning His Son required that He should be born(8) of a virgin, why should He not have received of the virgin the body which He bore from the virgin? Because, (forsooth) it is something else which He took from God, for "the Word "say they, "was made flesh."(9) Now this very statement plainly shows what it was that was made flesh; nor can it possibly be that(10) anything else than the Word was made flesh. Now, whether it was of the flesh that the Word was made flesh, or whether it was so made of the (divine) seed itself, the Scripture must tell us. As, however, the Scripture is silent about everything except what it was that was made (flesh), and says nothing of that from which it was so made, it must be held to suggest that from something else, and not from itself, was the Word made flesh. And if not from itself, but from something else, from what can we more suitably suppose that the Word became flesh than from that flesh in which it submitted to the dispensation?(11) And (we have a proof of the same conclusion in the fact) that the Lord Himself sententiously and distinctly pronounced, "that which is born of the flesh is flesh,"(12) even because it is born of the flesh. But if He here spoke of a human being simply, and not of Himself, (as you maintain) then you must deny absolutely that Christ is man, and must maintain that human nature was not suitable to Him. And then He adds, "That which is born of the Spirit is spirit,"(13) because God is a Spirit, and He was born of God. Now this description is certainly even more applicable to Him than it is to those who believe in Him. But if this passage indeed apply to Him, then why does not the preceding one also? For you cannot divide their relation, and adapt this to Him, and the previous clause to all other men, especially as you do not deny that Christ possesses the two substances, both of the flesh and of the Spirit. Besides, as He was in possession both of flesh and of Spirit, He cannot possibly, when speaking of the condition of the two substances which He Himself bears, be supposed to have determined that the Spirit indeed was His own, but that the flesh was not His own. Forasmuch, therefore, as He is of the Spirit He is God the Spirit, and is born of God; just as He is also born of the flesh of man, being generated in the flesh as man.(14)

CHAP. XIX.—CHRIST, AS TO HIS DIVINE NATURE, AS THE WORD OF GOD, BECAME FLESH, NOT BY CARNAL CONCEPTION, NOR BY THE WILL OF THE FLESH AND OF MAN, BUT BY THE WILL OF GOD. CHRIST'S DIVINE NATURE, OF ITS OWN ACCORD, DESCENDED INTO THE VIRGIN'S WOMB.

What, then, is the meaning of this passage, "Born's not of blood, nor of the will of the flesh, nor of the will of man, but of God?"(16) I shall make more use of this passage after I have confuted those who have tampered with it. They maintain that it was written thus (in the plural)(17)" Who were born, not of blood, nor of the will of the flesh, nor of the will of man, but of God," as if designating those who were before mentioned as "believing in His name," in order to point out the existence of that mysterious seed of the elect and spiritual which they appropriate to themselves.(18) But how can this be, when all who believe in the name of the Lord are, by reason of the common principle of the human race, born of blood, and of the will of the flesh, and of man, as indeed is Valentinus himself? The expression is in the singular number, as referring to the Lord, "He was born of God." And very properly, because Christ is the Word of God, and with the Word the Spirit of God, and by the Spirit the Power of God, and whatsoever else appertains to God. As flesh, however, He is not of blood, nor of the will of the flesh, nor of man, because it was by the will of God that the Word was made flesh. To the flesh, indeed, and not to the Word, accrues the denial of the nativity which is natural to us all as men,(1) because it was as flesh that He had thus to be born, and not as the Word. Now, whilst the passage actually denies that He was born of the will of the flesh, how is it that it did not also deny (that He was born) of the substance of the flesh? For it did not disavow the substance of the flesh when it denied His being "born of blood" but only the matter of the seed,' which, as all know, is the warm blood as convected by ebullition(2) into the coagulum of the woman's blood. In the cheese, it is from the coagulation that the milky substance acquires that consistency,(3) which is condensed by infusing the rennet.(4) We thus understand that what is denied is the Lord's birth after sexual intercourse (as is suggested by the phrase, "the will of man and of the flesh"), not His nativity from a woman's womb. Why, too, is it insisted on with such an accumulation of emphasis that He was not born of blood, nor of the will of the flesh, nor (of the will) of man, if it were not that His flesh was such that no man could have any doubt on the point of its being born from sexual intercourse? Again, although denying His birth from such cohabitation, the passage did not deny that He was born of real flesh; it rather affirmed this, by the very fact that it did not deny His birth in the flesh in the same way that it denied His birth from sexual intercourse. Pray, tell me, why the Spirit of Gods descended into a woman's womb at all, if He did not do so for the purpose of partaking of flesh from the womb. For He could have become spiritual flesh(6) without such a process,—much more simply, indeed, without the womb than in it. He had no reason for enclosing Himself within one, if He was to bear forth nothing from it. Not without reason, however, did He descend into a womb. Therefore He received (flesh) therefrom; else, if He received nothing therefrom, His descent into it would have been without a reason, especially if He meant to become flesh of that sort which was not derived from a womb, that is to say, a spiritual one.(7)

CHAP. XX.—CHRIST BORN OF A VIRGIN, OF HER SUBSTANCE. THE PHYSIOLOGICAL FACTS OF HIS REAL AND EXACT BIRTH OF A HUMAN MOTHER, AS SUGGESTED BY CERTAIN PASSAGES OF SCRIPTURE.

But to what shifts you resort, in your attempt to rob the syllable ex (of)(8) of its proper force as a preposition, and to substitute another for it in a sense not found throughout the Holy Scriptures! You say that He was born through a virgin, not of" a virgin, and in a womb, not of a womb, because the angel in the dream said to Joseph, "That which is born in her" (not of her) "is of the Holy Ghost."(11) But the fact is, if he had meant "of her," he must have said "in her;" for that which was of her, was also in her. The angel's expression, therefore, "in her," has precisely the same meaning as the phrase "of her." It is, however, a fortunate circumstance that Matthew also, when tracing down the Lord's descent from Abraham to Mary, says, "Jacob begat Joseph the husband of Mary, of whom was born Christ."(12) But Paul, too, silences these critics(13) when he says, "God sent forth His Son, made of a woman."(14) Does he mean through a woman, or in a woman? Nay more, for the sake of greater emphasis, he uses the word "made" rather than born, although the use of the latter expression would have been simpler. But by saying "made," he not only confirmed the statement, "The Word was made flesh,"(15) but he also asserted the reality of the flesh which was made of a virgin We shall have also the support of the Psalms on this point,not the "Psalms" indeed of Valentinus the apostate, and heretic, and Platonist, but the Psalms of David, the most illustrious saint and well−known prophet. He sings to us of Christ, and through his voice Christ indeed also sang concerning Himself. Hear, then, Christ the Lord speaking to God the Father: "Thou art He that didst draw(16) me out of my

mother's womb."(1) Here is the first point. "Thou art my hope from my mother's breasts; upon Thee have I been cast from the womb."(2) Here is another point. "Thou art my God from my mother's belly."(3) Here is a third point. Now let us carefully attend to the sense of these passages. "Thou didst draw me," He says, "out of the womb." Now what is it which is drawn, if it be not that which adheres, that which is firmly fastened to anything from which it is drawn in order to be sundered? If He clove not to the womb, how could He have been drawn from it? If He who clove thereto was drawn from it, how could He have adhered to it, if it were not that, all the while He was in the womb, He was tied to it, as to His origin,(4) by the umbilical cord, which communicated growth to Him from the matrix? Even when one strange matter amalgamates with another, it becomes so entirely incorporated(5) with that with which it amalgamates, that when it is drawn off from it, it carries with it some part of the body from which it is torn, as if in consequence of the severance of the union and growth which the constituent pieces had communicated to each other. But what were His "mother's breasts" which He mentions? No doubt they were those which He sucked. Midwives, and doctors, and naturalists, can tell us, from the nature of women's breasts, whether they usually flow at any other time than when the womb is affected with pregnancy, when the veins convey therefrom the blood of the lower parts(6) to the mamilla, and in the act of transference convert the secretion into the nutritious(7) substance of milk. Whence it comes to pass that during the period of lactation the monthly issues are suspended. But if the Word was made flesh of Himself without any communication with a womb, no mother's womb operating upon Him with its usual function and support, how could the lacteal fountain have been conveyed (from the womb) to the breasts, since (the womb) can only effect the change by actual possession of the proper substance? But it could not possibly have had blood for transformation into milk, unless it possessed the causes of blood also, that is to say, the severance (by birth)(8) of its own flesh from the mother's womb. Now it is easy to see what was the novelty of Christ's being born of a virgin. It was simply this, that (He was born) of a virgin in the real manner which we have indicated, in order that our regeneration might have virginal purity,—spiritually cleansed from all pollutions through Christ, who was Himself a virgin, even in the flesh, in that He was born of a virgin's flesh.

CHAP. XXI.—THE WORD OF GOD DID NOT BECOME FLESH EXCEPT IN THE VIRGIN'S WOMB AND OF HER SUBSTANCE. THROUGH HIS MOTHER HE IS DESCENDED FROM HER GREAT ANCESTOR DAVID.

HE IS DESCRIBED BOTH IN THE OLD AND IN THE NEW TESTAMENT AS "THE FRUIT OF DAVID'S LOINS."

Whereas, then, they contend that the novelty (of Christ's birth) consisted in this, that as the Word of God became flesh without the seed of a human father, so there should be no flesh of the virgin mother (assisting in the transaction), why should not the novelty rather be confined to this, that His flesh, although not born of seed, should yet have proceeded from flesh? I should like to go more closely into this discussion. "Behold," says he, "a virgin shall conceive in the womb."(9) Conceive what? I ask. The Word of God, of course, and not the seed of man, and in order, certainly, to bring forth a son. "For," says he, "she shall bring forth a son."(10) Therefore, as the act of conception was her own,(11) so also what she brought forth was her own, also, although the cause of conception(12) was not. If, on the other hand, the Word became flesh of Himself, then He both conceived and brought forth Himself, and the prophecy is stultified. For in that case a virgin did not conceive, and did not bring forth; since whatever she brought forth from the conception of the Word, is not her own flesh. But is this the only statement of prophecy which will be frustrated?(13) Will not the angel's announcement also be subverted, that the virgin should "conceive in her womb and bring forth a son?"(14) And will not in fact every scripture which declares that Christ had a mother? For how could she have been His mother, unless He had been in her womb? But then He received nothing from her womb which could make her a mother in whose womb He had been.(15) Such a name as this(16) a strange flesh ought not to assume. No flesh can speak of a mother's womb but that which is itself the offspring of that womb; nor can any be the offspring of the said womb if it owe its birth solely to itself. Therefore even Elisabeth must be silent although she is carrying in her womb the prophetic babe, which was already conscious of his Lord, and is, moreover, filled with the Holy Ghost.(1) For without reason does she say, "and whence is this to me that the mother of my Lord should come to me?"(2) If it was not as her son, but only as a stranger that Mary carried Jesus in her womb, how is it she says, "Blessed is the fruit of thy womb?(3) What is this fruit of the womb, which received not its germ from the womb, which had not its root in the womb, which belongs not to her whose is the womb, and which is no doubt the real fruit of the womb—even Christ? Now, since He is the blossom of the stem which sprouts from the root of Jesse; since, moreover, the root of Jesse is the family of David, and the stem of the root is Mary descended from David, and the blossom of the stem is Mary's son, who is called Jesus Christ, will not He also be the fruit? For the blossom is the fruit, because through the blossom and from the blossom every product advances from its rudimental condition(4) to perfect fruit. What then? They, deny to the fruit its blossom, and to the blossom its stem, and to the stem its root; so that the root fails to secures for itself, by means of the stem, that special product which comes from the stem, even the blossom and the fruit; for every step indeed in a genealogy is traced from the latest up to the first, so that it is now a well-known fact that the flesh of Christ is inseparable,(6) not merely from Mary, but also from David through Mary, and from Jesse through David. "This fruit," therefore, "of David's loins," that is to say, of his posterity in the flesh, God swears to him that "He will raise up to sit upon his throne."(7) If "of David's loins," how much rather is He of Mary's loins, by virtue of whom He is in "the loins of David?"

CHAP. XXII.—HOLY SCRIPTURE IN THE NEW TESTAMENT, EVEN IN ITS VERY FIRST VERSE, TESTIFIES TO CHRIST'S TRUE FLESH. IN VIRTUE OF WHICH HE IS INCORPORATED IN THE HUMAN STOCK OF DAVID, AND ABRAHAM, AND ADAM.

They may, then, obliterate the testimony of the devils which proclaimed Jesus the son of David; but whatever unworthiness there be in this testimony, that of the apostles they will never be able to efface, There is, first of all, Matthew, that most faithful chronicler(8) of the Gospel, because the companion of the Lord; for no other reason in the world than to show us clearly the fleshly original(9) of Christ, he thus begins his Gospel: "The book of the generation of Jesus Christ, the son of David, the son of Abraham."(10) With a nature issuing from such fountal sources, and an order gradually descending to the birth of Christ, what else have we here described than the very flesh of Abraham and of David conveying itself down, step after step, to the very virgin, and at last introducing

Christ,—nay, producing Christ Himself of the virgin? Then, again, there is Paul, who was at once both a disciple, and a master, and a witness of the selfsame Gospel; as an apostle of the same Christ, also, he affirms that Christ "was made of the seed of David, according to the flesh,"(11)—which, therefore, was His own likewise. Christ's flesh, then, is of David's seed. Since He is of the seed of David in consequence of Mary's flesh, He is therefore of Mary's flesh because of the seed of David. In what way so ever you torture the statement, He is either of the flesh of Mary because of the seed of David, or He is of the seed of David because of the flesh of Mary. The whole discussion is terminated by the same apostle, when he declares Christ to be "the seed of Abraham." And if of Abraham, how much more, to be sure, of David, as a more recent progenitor! For, unfolding the promised blessing upon all nations in the person(12) of Abraham, "And in thy seed shall all nations of the earth be blessed," he adds, "He saith not, And to seeds, as of many; but as of one, And to thy seed, which is Christ."(13) When we read and believe these things, what sort of flesh ought we, and can we, acknowledge in Christ? Surely none other than Abraham's, since Christ is "the seed of Abraham;" none other than Jesse's, since Christ is the blossom of "the stem of Jesse;" none other than David's, since Christ is "the fruit of David's loins;" none other than Mary's, since Christ came from Mary's womb; and, higher still, none other than Adam's, since Christ is "the second Adam." The consequence, therefore, is that they must either maintain, that those (ancestors) had a spiritual flesh, that so there might be derived to Christ the same condition of substance, or else allow that the flesh of Christ was not a spiritual one, since it is not traced from the origin(14) of a spiritual stock.

CHAP. XXIII.—SIMEON'S "SIGN THAT SHOULD BE CONTRADICTED," APPLIED TO THE HERETICAL GAINSAYING OF THE TRUE BIRTH OF CHRIST. ONE OF THE HERETICS' PARADOXES TURNED IN SUPPORT OF CATHOLIC TRUTH.

We acknowledge, however, that the prophetic declaration of Simeon is fulfilled, which he spoke over the recently–born Saviour:(1) "Behold, this child is set for the fall and rising again of many in Israel, and for a sign that shall be spoken against."(2) The sign (here meant) is that of the birth of Christ, according to Isaiah: "Therefore the Lord Himself shall give you a sign: behold, a virgin shall conceive and bear a son."(3) We discover, then, what the sign is which is to be spoken against—the conception and the parturition of the Virgin Mary, concerning which these sophists(4) say: "She a virgin and yet not a virgin bare, and yet did not bear;" just as if such language, if indeed it must be uttered, would not be more suitable even for ourselves to use! For "she bare," because she produced offspring of her own flesh and "yet she did not bear," since she produced Him not from a husband's seed; she was "a virgin," so far as (abstinence) from a husband went, and "yet not a virgin," as regards her bearing a child. There is not, however, that parity of reasoning which the heretics affect: in other words it does not follow that for the reason "she did not bear,"(5) she who was "not a virgin" was "yet a virgin," even because she became a mother without any fruit of her own womb. But with us there is no equivocation, nothing twisted into a double sense.(6) Light is light; and darkness, darkness; yea is yea; and nay, nay; "whatsoever is more than these cometh of evil."(7) She who bare (really) bare; and although she was a virgin when she conceived, she was a wife(8) when she brought forth her son. Now, as a wife, she was under the very law of "opening the womb,"(9) wherein it was quite immaterial whether the birth of the male was by virtue of a husband's co−operation or not;(10) it was the same sex(11) that opened her womb. Indeed, hers is the womb on account of which it is written of others also: "Every male that openeth the womb shall be called holy to the Lord."(12) For who is really holy but the Son of God? Who properly opened the womb but He who opened a closed one?(13) But it is marriage which opens the womb in all cases. The virgin's womb, therefore, was especially(14) opened, because it was especially closed. Indeed(15) she ought rather to be called not a virgin than a virgin, becoming a mother at a leap, as it were, before she was a wife. And what must be said more on this point? Since it was in this sense that the apostle declared that the Son of God was born not of a virgin, but "of a woman," he in that statement recognised the condition of the "opened womb" which ensues in marriage.(16) We read in Ezekiel of "a heifer(17) which brought forth, and still did not bring forth." Now, see whether it was not in view of your own future contentions about the womb of Mary, that even then the Holy Ghost set His mark upon you in this passage; otherwise(18) He would not, contrary to His usual simplicity of style (in this prophet), have uttered a sentence of such doubtful import, especially when Isaiah says, "She shall conceive and bear a son."(19)

CHAP. XXIV.—DIVINE STRICTURES ON VARIOUS HERETICS DESCRIED IN VARIOUS PASSAGES OF PROPHETICAL SCRIPTURE. THOSE WHO ASSAIL THE TRUE DOCTRINE OF THE ONE LORD JESUS CHRIST, BOTH GOD AND MAN, THUS CONDEMNED.

For when Isaiah hurls denunciation against our very heretics, especially in his "Woe to them that call evil good, and put darkness for light,"(20) he of course sets his mark upon those amongst you(21) who preserve not in the words they employ the light of their true significance, (by taking care) that the soul should mean only that which is so called, and the flesh simply that which is confest to our view and God none other than the One who is preached.(22) Having thus Marcion in his prophetic view, he says, "I am God, and there is none else; there is no God beside me."(23) And when in another passage he says, in like manner, "Before me there was no God,"(24) he strikes at those inexplicable genealogies of the Valentinian AEons. Again, there is an answer to Ebion in the Scripture: "Born,(25) not of blood, nor of the will of the flesh, nor of the will of man, but of God." In like manner, in the passage, "If even an angel of heaven preach unto you any other gospel than that which we have preached unto you, let him be anathema,"(1) he calls attention to the artful influence of Philumene,(2) the virgin friend of Apelles. Surely he is antichrist who denies that Christ has come in the flesh.(3) By declaring that His flesh is simply and absolutely true, and taken in the plain sense of its own nature, the Scripture aims a blow at all who make distinctions in it.(4) In the same way, also, when it defines the very Christ to be but one, it shakes the fancies of those who exhibit a multiform Christ, who make Christ to be one being and Jesus another,—representing one as escaping out of the midst of the crowds, and the other as detained by them; one as appearing on a solitary mountain to three companions, clothed with glory in a cloud, the other as an ordinary man holding intercourse with all,(5) one as magnanimous, but the other as timid; lastly, one as suffering death, the other as risen again, by means of which event they maintain a resurrection of their own also, only in another flesh. Happily, however, He who suffered "will come again from heaven,"(6) and by all shall He be seen, who rose again from the dead. They too who crucified Him shall see and acknowledge Him; that is to say, His very flesh, against which they spent their fury, and without which it would be impossible for Himself either to exist or to be seen; so that they must blush with shame who affirm that His flesh sits in heaven void of sensation, like a sheath only, Christ being withdrawn from it; as well as those who (maintain) that His flesh and soul are just the same thing,(7) or else that His soul is all that exists? but that His flesh no longer lives.

CHAP. XXV.—CONCLUSION.THIS TREATISE FORMS A PREFACE TO THE OTHER WORK, "ON "PROVING THE RESURRECTION OF THE FLESH," THE REALITY OF THE FLESH WHICH WAS TRULY BORN, AND DIED, AND ROSE AGAIN.

But let this suffice on our present subject; for I think that by this time proof enough has been adduced of the flesh in Christ having both been born of the virgin, and being human in its nature. And this discussion alone might have been sufficient, without encountering the isolated opinions which have been raised from different quarters. We have, however, challenged these opinions to the test, both of the arguments which sustain them, and of the Scriptures which are appealed to,and this we have done ex abundanti; so that we have, by showing what the flesh of Christ was, and whence it was derived, also predetermined the question, against all objectors, of what that flesh was not. The resurrection, however, of our own flesh will have to be maintained in another little treatise, and so bring to a close this present one, which serves as a general preface, and which will pave the way far the approaching subject now that it is plain what kind of body that was which rose again in Christ.

ELUCIDATIONS.

I. (In the body of a dove, cap. iii. p. 523.)

The learned John Scott, in his invaluable work The Christian Life,(1) identifies the glory shed upon the Saviour at his baptism, with that mentioned by Ezekiel (Cap. xliii. 2) and adds: "In this same glorious splendor was Christ arrayed first at his Baptism and afterward at his Transfiguration .... By the Holy Ghost's descending like a Dove, it is not necessary we should understand his descending in the shape or form of a Dove, but that in some glorious form, or appearance, he descended in the same manner as a Dove descends .... Came down from above just as a dove with his wings spread forth is observed to do, and lighted upon our Saviour's head." I quote this as the opinion of one of the most learned and orthodox of divines, but not as my own, for I cannot reconcile it, as he strives to do, with St. Luke iii. 22. Compare Justin Martyr, vol. i. p. 243, and note 6, this series.

Grotius observes, says Dr. Scott, that in the apocryphal Gospel of the Nazarenes, it is said that at the Baptism of our Lord "a great light shone round about the place."

II.

(His mother and His brethren, cap. vii. p. 527.)

It is not possible that the author of this chapter had ever conceived of the Blessed Virgin otherwise than as "Blessed among women," indeed, but enjoying no especial prerogative as the mother of our Lord. He speaks of "denying her" and "putting her away" after He began His Ministry, as He requires His ministers to do, after His example. How extraordinary this language— "the repudiation of carnal relationship." According to our author, never charged with heresy on this

44

point, the high rewards of the holy Mary, in the world to come will he those due to her faith, not to the blessing of "her breasts and of her womb." Christ designates those as "more blessed," who hear His word and keep it. This the Blessed Virgin did pre–eminently, and herein was her own greater blessedness; that is, (our author shews) her crown of glory depends chiefly, like that of other saints, on her faith and works, not on her mere Maternity.

Printed in the United States
47747LVS00004B/12